D0886606

Tiger Woods

Read These Other
Ferguson Career Biographies

Maya Angelou
Author and
Documentary Filmmaker
by Lucia Raatma

Leonard Bernstein
Composer and Conductor
by Jean F. Blashfield

Shirley Temple Black
Actor and Diplomat
by Jean F. Blashfield

George Bush
Business Executive
and U.S. President
by Robert Green

Bill Gates
Computer Programmer
and Entrepreneur
by Lucia Raatma

John Glenn
Astronaut and U.S. Senator
by Robert Green

Martin Luther King Jr.
Minister and
Civil Rights Activist
by Brendan January

Charles Lindbergh
Pilot
by Lucia Raatma

Sandra Day O'Connor
Lawyer and
Supreme Court Justice
by Jean Kinney Williams

Wilma Rudolph
Athlete and Educator
by Alice K. Flanagan

Tiger
Woods

Professional Golfer

BY JEAN KINNEY WILLIAMS

Ferguson Publishing Company
Chicago, Illinois

Photographs ©: Archive/Reuters/Mike Blake, 8, 50, 105; Allsport/Steve Munday, 12; All-sport/Ken Levine, 14; Corbis/Bettmann/Agence France Presse, 17; Corbis/Alan Leven-son, 19, 34; Gamma Liaison/Laurent van der Stock, 24; Allsport/David Cannon, 26; Gamma Liaison/Jones, 28; Allsport/Steve Powell, 31; AP/Wide World Photos/Dan Currier, 38–39; AP/Wide World Photos/Eric Risberg, 41; Allsport/Rusty Jarrett, 43; AP/Wide World Photos/Curtis Compton, 46; Archive Photos/Reuters/Gary Hershorn, 53; Allsport/J.D. Cuban, 54–55, 62, 68, 76–77, 81; Archive Photos/Reuters/Colin Braley, 58; Allsport/Hul-ton Deutsch, 64–65; AP/Wide World Photos/Milwaukee Journal Sentinel/Benny Sieu, 72; AP/Wide World Photos/Don Ryan, 75; Archive Photos/Reuters/John Kuntz, 84; Archive Photos/Reuters/Mike Blake, 88; AP/Wide World Photos/Jay LaPrete, 90; All-sport/Jon Ferrey, 92–93; Archive Photos/Reuters/Charles W. Luzier, 96; Archive Photos, 98; AP/Wide World Photos/Kathy Willens, 100; Allsport/Donal Miralle, 107.

An Editorial Directions Book
Library of Congress Cataloging-in-Publication Data
Williams, Jean Kinney.
    Tiger Woods : professional golfer / by Jean Kinney Williams.
    p. cm. — (Ferguson career biographies)
    Includes bibliographical references and index.
    ISBN 0-89434-371-8
    1. Woods, Tiger—Juvenile literature. 2. Golfers—United States—Biography—Juvenile literature. [1. Woods, Tiger. 2. Golfers. 3. Racially mixed people—Biography.] I. Title. II. Series.
GV964.W66 W56 2001
796.352'092—dc21
[B]   00-066262

Printed in the United States of America
Y-3

CONTENTS

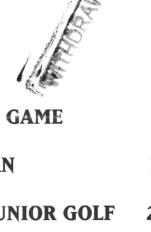

Tiger Woods

A winning smile. Tiger Woods's presence has made golf more popular than ever.

CHANGING THE GAME

The year 1996 was a year of change in the staid old game of golf. That year, a young man from California announced that he intended to become a professional golfer, and the game hasn't been the same since. In fact, you might say Tiger Woods doubled the impact that most professional athletes would hope to have on their sport.

Woods not only brought an unusual racial heritage to a game dominated by white athletes, but he has also taken the game to new levels of excellence and popularity. Adults and young people of all backgrounds began turning up at his matches. Even other golf professionals were amazed at what Tiger Woods could do on a golf course. "Tiger has made it cool to be a golfer," said David Duval, his friend and often his rival.

Young Talent

Tiger was still an infant when his father, Earl Woods, introduced him to golf. He was swinging a club before he was even out of diapers. As he was growing up in Southern California, he strove to beat the records set by Jack Nicklaus, considered by many to be the best golfer ever. Now, in future decades, it will be the records set by Tiger Woods that young golfers will have to keep their eyes on.

Not only did Woods have a natural gift for golf that his father quickly recognized, but he also had a love for the game. His parents never had to force him to practice. In fact, they sometimes had to keep him from practicing too much.

A Focused Game

Another important quality Woods brings to his golf game is concentration. His opponents have learned that even when they're ahead of Tiger by several golf strokes, he can buckle down and focus intensely on what he needs to do on each shot. Not only is Woods likely to catch up to his opponent—there's a good chance he'll end up winning.

But perhaps what really sets Tiger Woods apart from other golfers is his confidence. He allows himself to take risks when other golfers tend to play it safe. For example, he might decide to try and drive the golf ball right over a stand of trees to reach the putting green sooner, while his opponents try to go around the trees. If a shot like that doesn't work, Woods finds a way to learn from it, rather than get angry with himself for trying it.

Woods really showed his self-confidence when he decided to change his golf swing only a year or so after turning pro. He didn't reach that decision because he'd been playing poor golf. In fact, he began to change his swing shortly after a major victory. In 1997, at age twenty-one, he became the youngest player ever to win the prestigious Masters Tournament, and he won it by twelve strokes, the largest margin ever.

But Tiger believed he could play even better golf if he improved his swing. For the next year and a half, he won no tournaments, and sometimes he felt

Pumped up. Woods enjoyed sinking a number of amazing putts for his first Masters win in 1997.

stung by the disappointment expressed by fans or the press. However, by the middle of 1999, when Woods got his new golf swing in gear, there seemed to be no stopping him.

Today, Tiger Woods is considered golf's best player ever. It isn't just reporters who call him *the* superstar of the international sports world. Basketball great Michael Jordan has called Woods one of *his* sports heroes. But Woods's arrival at this height of success was no accident.

Focused. Woods learned at an early age to concentrate when he played golf.

A TIGER IS BORN

I f it weren't for his determined mother, there might not be a Tiger Woods. Kultida Woods is a native of Thailand. She was a secretary in a United States Army office there when she met Earl Woods, an American officer who was stationed in Thailand in the late 1960s. Earl asked Kultida for a date, and they planned to meet at eight o'clock. Earl arrived at their meeting place at 8:00 in the evening, but saw no Kultida. She showed up at 8:00 the next morning and thought she, too, had been stood up.

She went looking for Earl. "We had a date," she reminded him when she found him.

"Yeah, last night," Earl answered. It was then he learned that young, single Thai women didn't go out with men at night by themselves.

"We still have a date," she insisted to Earl. Because it was a Buddhist holy day in Thailand, she asked him to take her to the Temple of the Reclining Buddha. Buddhism is the predominant religion in Thailand. That first date eventually led to a marriage proposal.

Tiger's Parents

Earl was a divorced father of three children when he married Kultida in 1969. They moved to Southern California when Earl retired from the army. He took a job with McDonnell Douglas, and the couple bought a home in nearby Cypress in Orange County, California.

The population of Cypress was mostly white. However, Earl Woods is half African-American, one-quarter Chinese, and one-quarter Native American. Kultida is half Thai, one-quarter Chinese, and one-quarter Caucasian. The Woodses soon discovered they weren't exactly welcome in Cypress. At first,

A proud mother. Kultida Woods helped make her son into the determined man he is today.

limes from local trees were thrown at their windows. Then their home became the target of BB guns. But the Woodses stayed put, and eventually the harassment ended.

Young Tiger

Earl and Kultida welcomed a son on December 30, 1975. They named him Eldrick, a name Kultida created from her and Earl's names. But from the beginning, his parents called him "Tiger," a nickname given in honor of a man who saved Earl's life in Vietnam years earlier.

During the 1960s, Earl served two tours of duty as a Green Beret in the Vietnam War. He worked closely with a South Vietnamese officer named Nguyen Phong. Twice Phong alerted Earl to what would have been deadly strikes—once by a North Vietnamese sniper and once by a poisonous snake. Earl called his friend "Tiger" because "he was a tiger in combat." The war ended two years after American soldiers left South Vietnam, when the North Vietnamese army overran South Vietnam. Though Earl hoped to keep in touch with his South Vietnamese friend, he never heard from him again. But he wanted to honor Phong by calling his own son "Tiger."

Earl Woods was a prominent baseball player in college at Kansas State University. However, when he was in his forties, he discovered another game he loved—golf. When Tiger was a baby, he would sit in his high chair and watch his father practice driving balls into a net. Kultida would try to feed Tiger, but he wanted to watch his father. So Earl would stop long enough for Tiger to eat a spoonful of food, then hit another shot. At ten months, when Tiger was still barely able to stand, he picked up a golf club that Earl had cut down to size and executed what

Father and son. Earl and Tiger Woods share a love for golf and a special bond.

looked like a perfect swing. Tiger smacked a golf ball into the net. "I was flabbergasted. I almost fell off my chair," Earl said later.

A Gift for Golf

Even at Tiger's young age, Earl realized his son had a gift for golf. He decided that he would do everything to encourage it, and from that point on, Tiger had little use for typical baby toys. His favorite "toys" were a vacuum-cleaner hose, which he pretended was a golf club, and a tennis ball. When he was eighteen months old, Tiger was trying out the driving range. He'd swing an iron club Earl had cut down for him and hit a bucket of golf balls before he was ready to go home, have a bottle, and take a nap. Then Earl let him try playing a hole at the U.S. Navy golf course in Cypress. It was a par-four hole (which means a good golfer should get the ball from the teeing-off point to the hole with four hits of the ball), and Tiger scored an 11. He took eight shots to get it to the putting green, then three putts to get it in the cup.

When Tiger was two years old, Kultida called a Los Angeles television sports anchor to tell him about her son's remarkable golf abilities. The TV station sent a camera crew to the golf course, and Tiger made the local news. A producer for "The Mike Douglas Show," a nationwide talk show, saw Tiger on the news, and invited him to be on the show along with golf-loving entertainer Bob Hope. They had a putting contest, and Tiger complained that the putting green wasn't level, much to the amusement of Mike Douglas and Bob Hope.

During another television interview, he was asked how he'd become such a good golfer. "Pwactice," he answered. How much did he practice? "About a whole bunch."

The U.S. Navy golf course had a rule that children under age ten couldn't play without an adult, so Kultida looked for another golf course where four-year-old Tiger could play anytime. She asked golf teacher and professional Rudy Duran at Heartwell Golf Park in Long Beach if Tiger could play the course there. Duran watched Tiger hit a few balls and was amazed. "It was unbelievable. He was awesome," Duran said of little Tiger's golf demonstration. Duran compared Tiger to Mozart, the musical genius who showed his talents at a very early age. Duran was happy to become Tiger's first golf teacher.

Tiger received his own full set of clubs when he was five. He scored in the 90s on regular eighteen-hole golf courses, a score comparable to that of many adult golfers. When Tiger was six, Rudy Duran took him to several golf clubs and parks to try a variety of courses. As he played challenging holes, Tiger might get himself into a tricky situation, such as hitting the ball into sand or woods. He would then try to figure his way out of it, deciding which club to use or just how to hit the ball without asking Duran for help or advice. Tiger could drive the ball more than 100 yards (91 meters). And by watching other golfers, he could analyze the strengths or weaknesses of their swings. He made another television appearance on the show "That's Incredible."

Off to School

By this time, Tiger was ready for kindergarten. Schoolwork came easily for him too. Just as Earl had introduced Tiger to golf at an early age, Kultida began teaching him addition when he was a toddler and then multiplication as he got older. His reward for working on math was a round of golf with his father in the afternoon.

Tiger's kindergarten year got off to a rough start, though. He was one of only a few minority students in his school and, on his first day, some older white students tied him to a tree. The older children were caught and punished, but Tiger had experienced his first brush with racism. His father taught him not to be bitter but to show the world what he could do with his golf clubs. Aside from that experience, Tiger enjoyed school and interacting with other children. His kindergarten teacher even recommended that he be advanced to first grade, but Tiger wanted to stay where he was. In golf, he was always playing with or against older children, and in school he enjoyed being with other six-year-olds. So Tiger remained in kindergarten.

He continued to do well as his parents emphasized schoolwork before golf. Kultida found that if Tiger needed discipline, taking away his golf cubs was very effective punishment. "He stays in line pretty good that way," she said. Homework always had to be finished—and done correctly—before he could practice or play golf. But summers meant long days on the golf course for Tiger, with no schoolwork to worry about. Earl and Kultida still didn't have to tell him to practice his sport. Instead, they had to pressure him to come home from the golf course.

Happy to practice. A young Tiger Woods had to be reminded to tend to responsibilities other than golf.

A Good Sport

His parents also stressed the importance of sportsmanship. Once Tiger played a round of golf with Steward Reed, a professional golfer. He was beating Reed for the first nine holes, but then Reed caught up and won the match. Tiger, in tears, refused to shake hands with Reed. He received quite a scolding from Kultida, who told him, "You must be a sportsman, win or lose." She would also reprimand him for displays of bad temper.

Even when Tiger was off the golf course, Earl found a way to boost his son's confidence and mental attitude for the game. Earl bought tape recordings featuring sounds from nature, like flowing river water, with recorded messages such as, "I will my own destiny. I smile at obstacles. I focus and give it my all." Tiger listened to them at bedtime until eventually the tapes wore out.

You might say Tiger had his first taste of professional golf at age six, when he played a two-hole match with golf champion Sam Snead. Snead beat him by one stroke. At one point, Tiger's ball landed on the edge of a pond, and Snead suggested that he just take the shot over. But Duran never gave Tiger any special advantages when they played. So Tiger

Golf pro Sam Snead. When Woods was just six years old, he and Snead played a two-hole match.

played the ball from where it lay, and he got it back up on the green. After their "match," Snead and Tiger exchanged autographs. He was still just six years old, but giving out autographs and playing golf against professionals would become a way of life for Tiger in years to come.

Team Tiger. Earl Woods made sure that his son was surrounded by good coaches and other supportive people.

DOMINATING
JUNIOR GOLF

Tiger entered his first international tournament at age six. He came in eighth out of 150 contestants, but lost only to ten-year-olds. When he was eight, he won his first Optimist Junior World Championship. After he won that tournament again, at age nine and age twelve, Earl decided it was time to seek out more challenges for Tiger. Earl retired from his job, and the family lived on his pension while Earl and Tiger traveled to tournaments around the country. With airfare and hotel bills to cover (not to mention paying the coach), raising a golf champion was expensive. Eventually, the United States Golf Association (USGA) changed its rules so that junior golfers could accept money from tournament sponsors to pay those costs. That was good news for Earl and Kultida Woods, who at one point were spending almost $20,000 a year on Tiger's golf expenses.

When Tiger was ten years old, *Golf Digest* magazine printed a list of the lifetime achievements of legendary golfer Jack Nicklaus. Tiger cut it out and, over the years, he compared his own golf progress with Nicklaus's. Tiger read that Nicklaus was thirteen when he first scored lower than 70 on eighteen holes of golf. Tiger achieved that goal at age twelve. Nicklaus won his first U.S. Amateur tournament at age nineteen—Tiger would strive to beat that.

Team Tiger

Earl Woods was determined to groom Tiger for future golf championship. He hired a "team" of professionals to accomplish that. When Tiger was ten, his father hired John Anselmo as a new coach. Then Earl hired sports psychologist Jay Brunza to work with Tiger on mental techniques. Brunza used hypnosis, for example, which helped Tiger learn to keep

Golf legend Jack Nicklaus. As Tiger Woods grew up, he considered Nicklaus to be a role model.

focused on what he wanted to do at each shot in a game.

Earl also came up with a way to exercise Tiger's concentration skills. Earl would do something annoying or distracting just as Tiger was ready to take a swing or putt the ball. He might noisily undo the Velcro on his golf glove, flick his cigarette lighter at just the "right" moment, or step in front of Tiger's line of vision as Tiger began his swing. Sometimes Earl would even obviously cheat when playing against Tiger. Earl figured that sooner or later his son would face opponents who would try anything to win. He wanted Tiger to be able to deal with those situations without losing his concentration. Earl sometimes made Tiger furious during these mental "exercises," but they worked. Eventually Tiger learned to tune out distractions as he played and to stay focused on his golf game, no matter what.

Early Success

By age fourteen, Tiger won a fifth Junior World Optimist Championship, and he could drive the ball 300 yards (275 m). He was still in junior high school when he received a friendly letter from the golf coach at Stanford University in California, a college he was already interested in. By now he'd had his braces taken off, and his glasses were replaced with contact lenses. He was beginning to look like the smiling young man who would appear on magazine covers in a few more years.

Tiger probably had Jack Nicklaus's lifetime statistics memorized when they first met in 1991 at a Los Angeles golf tournament. After a day spent on the golf course, Nicklaus told him, "When I grow up, I hope my swing is as pretty as yours." That summer Tiger won his sixth Junior World Optimist Championship.

Next came the Junior U.S. Amateur Championship in Orlando, Florida. His final match in the tournament came down to a sudden-death playoff, and he showed the results of his mental training. He saved a bad hit off the tee, got the ball back on the green, and won the match by one stroke. "The pressure was awesome," he said after becoming the youngest winner of the tournament. By winning that championship, he was automatically entered in the U.S. Amateur Tournament, the youngest junior to enter it since 1916. But in the first two rounds, he failed to make the cut of players who continued for the rest of the tournament. It was an honor, though,

Eye on the ball. Woods spent time mastering all of the aspects of his golf game.

at age sixteen to be chosen as the American Junior Golf Association's Player of the Year in January 1992. At this point, Tiger could call himself the best junior golfer in the United States.

He and Earl began to look at tournament invitations more selectively as Tiger's prominence grew. Meanwhile, Tiger kept an A average in high school, and he still had to finish his homework before he played golf. In February 1992, he received a sponsor's exemption, or an invitation from the tournament sponsor, to play in the Los Angeles Open, an important event on the PGA (Professional Golfers' Association) Tour. Tiger received permission to miss classes to play in the tournament. He also received death threats because of his race. Extra security was added as he attempted to qualify for play after the Thursday and Friday rounds, but he didn't make the final cut.

That year, he still had another goal—to be the first to win two consecutive Junior U.S. Amateur Championships. The 1992 tournament was held in suburban Boston. While there, Tiger and Earl held a golf clinic for inner-city Boston youths. They held such workshops occasionally, hoping to spark interest in golf among other minority youths. But Tiger grew weary of the attention that often seemed more focused on his race than on his golf. He would point out that he wasn't only African-American, but descended from several races. He sometimes referred to himself as Asian-American instead of African-American. But when he won the Junior U.S. Amateur Championship that summer, no doubt there were many minority youths cheering him on. Again he was invited to participate in the U.S. Amateur, and again he didn't make the final cut. But among the older and more experienced golfers, his confidence was increasing.

One part of school that Tiger always enjoyed, whether in high school or college, was just being another student. He liked to think of himself as a "normal kid who happens to play golf pretty well," as he told one interviewer. But he didn't socialize as much or play a variety of sports like other boys his age did. Instead, he channeled most of his free time into practicing and playing golf, though he did enjoy track and field for a brief period. And though his golf was beyond that of his teammates in high school and college, he always liked being with his peers. He was a typical teenager in his diet, though—he would have been happy to eat nothing but McDonald's Big Macs and french fries. So, to keep fit, he developed an exercise program for himself that he borrowed from *Golf Digest.*

Getting Attention

As Tiger played in more PGA tournaments, he became better acquainted with several pros. They warned him to take things slow and not to rush into a professional golf career. Tiger was told he would benefit from playing golf at the college level before becoming a professional. "The golf world is littered with players" who shone at the junior level, "then vanished," says John Strege in *Tiger: A Biography of Tiger Woods*. Of the twenty-six players who won the Junior Amateur title in the years before Tiger, only three won any PGA events as professionals, Strege wrote. But, in general, most professionals thought Tiger Woods would be around for many years. The International Management Group (IMG), a company that manages the careers of professional athletes around the world, also had confidence in Tiger. When he was only sixteen, IMG began talking to him about managing his professional career when the time came.

In 1992, Tiger was invited to participate in the

Los Angeles Open, an event he'd been watching and attending for years. As golf's "boy wonder," Tiger was beginning to draw his own fans to tournaments. He'd also learned one trick of the professional trade:

Sharpie in hand. Woods has always been happy to sign autographs for his fans.

he carried a Sharpie pen, which could write on anything, to sign autographs.

Tiger still wasn't able to make the cut for final PGA tournament rounds, but he continued to gain experience and mental "conditioning" from exposure to the professional events. In 1993, he won a third consecutive Junior Amateur Championship, the first golfer to do so. In his come-from-behind win, he sent the match into a sudden-death playoff. Then his opponent bogeyed—hit one stroke over par—giving Tiger the match.

Amateur Champ

In 1994, Tiger was eighteen and finishing high school. He had a new coach, Houston golf pro Butch Harmon, who also had worked with Greg Norman. Usually Harmon coached Tiger over the phone and by videotape. Woods set a new goal for himself that year: to win the U.S. Amateur. If he did, he would be the youngest winner ever—and the first African-American. First he played in a professional tournament in his mother's native Thailand. Golf champions Greg Norman and Fred Couples were playing there too. For the first time, Tiger made the cut in a professional tournament, and he came in thirty-fourth. He also was eligible to qualify for the U.S. Open, a major golf tournament, but he skipped that. He wanted to attend his high school graduation ceremony instead.

Perfecting the swing. Butch Harmon offered great advice to Woods as he worked on his techniques.

That summer he played in—and won—a variety of adult-amateur tournaments, including the important Western Amateur in Michigan. When he arrived in Florida for the U.S. Amateur competition, he believed a win there would confirm his status as the country's best amateur golfer. He advanced through the first rounds of play, and during one match he called Butch Harmon to get advice on his swing. When he reached the final round, Tiger's opponent was college student Trip Kuehne. Kuehne led by five strokes after nineteen holes. This time it was Earl who gave advice to Tiger: "Let the legend grow," he said quietly in his son's ear. That bit of inspiration, it seemed, was as helpful as a swing correction from Harmon. Over the next fifteen holes Tiger made up his score deficit, tied up the score, and then won on the final hole. After congratulating Kuehne, he turned to his father. Both Earl and Tiger were in tears as they hugged. As the youngest champion ever of that tournament, Tiger beat another one of Jack Nicklaus's statistics.

At age eighteen, preparing to enter Stanford University in the fall and savoring his U.S. Amateur win, Tiger could now consider himself the best amateur golfer in the United States. The town of Cypress pre-

*Success! In 1994, Tiger Woods won his first U.S. Amateur
Championship title.*

sented him with the key to the city—the Woods family had come a long way from the days when limes were thrown at their windows. He began receiving loads of fan mail after his U.S. Amateur win including a letter from President Bill Clinton, which Kultida had framed.

"I commend you for the sportsmanship, discipline, and perseverance that earned you this great honor. Best wishes for every success at Stanford," President Clinton's letter said. Tiger's "junior" days were over as he headed for college and prepared to enter golf at the next level.

PLAYING AT THE NEXT LEVEL

4

iger entered Stanford University on a golf scholarship in the fall of 1994 and intended to study economics. He'd become a nationally known golfer, but he discovered there were lots of "stars" at Stanford, including young television actors, Olympic athletes, and of course, scholarly "champs." Stanford is an academically challenging university attended by students who were tops in their high school classes. "When I was in high school, I set the curve. Here, I follow it," Tiger said about his new school. "Everybody here is special in some way."

A Stanford student. Woods learned a lot about golf and a lot about himself during his college years.

Student Life

With all the attention he received on the golf course, he enjoyed being a "regular" student. He joined a fraternity, and his new friends found that he was an awful dancer. He might have had a golf swing admired by the world's best golfers, but on the dance floor, "his rhythm was terrible. He's got body parts going everywhere," joked one friend. And though he was accustomed to staying in good hotels when traveling to tournaments, as a freshman on Stanford's team he got a rollaway cot when the team traveled. That was fine with Tiger. He put as much effort into studying golf, such as watching videotaped tournaments, as he did his schoolwork, and his golf teammates often asked his advice on the game.

Facing Racism

One of the first matches the Stanford golf team played that year was an invitational tournament in Birmingham, Alabama. It was held at the Shoal Creek Country Club, site of a golf controversy just a few years earlier. In 1990, Shoal Creek was to host the PGA Championship. But the club didn't allow African-American members. Hall Thompson, the club's founder, said that having black members join a traditionally white-only golf club "just isn't done in Birmingham." Shoal Creek had other members who represented a variety of ethnic groups, but no African-Americans. "We can pick and choose who we want" as members, Thompson said in his defense. An African-American man was admitted to the club as a member shortly after sponsors threatened to boycott the PGA Championship.

Four years later, when the Stanford team arrived there for a tournament, some protesters thought Tiger should boycott the match. As if to defy both the protesters and whatever racism still lingered there, Tiger scored a 67 and won the tournament. Club-owner Thompson, who didn't want African-American members a few years earlier, congratulated Tiger and shook his hand.

Soon after returning to campus from the Alabama tournament, Tiger was mugged by a robber who called him by name: "Tiger, give me your wallet," he was told. Tiger didn't have a wallet with him, but the mugger took his gold necklace and watch, then hit Tiger's jaw with the handle of a knife. Tiger was all right physically, but he had to wonder if he'd been singled out because he was a minority champion in a traditionally all-white sport. He'd also received a racist letter that fall when he first arrived on campus.

Playing the Masters

Again, as his parents taught him to do, Tiger used his golf clubs to silence his critics. Having won the U.S. Amateur, he was allowed to enter the Masters tournament in Augusta, Georgia, the following spring. The Masters is one of the Grand Slam tournaments that professional golfers strive to win; it's considered quite an honor to don the green jacket that is awarded each year to the winner. The other Grand Slam tournaments on the professional golf circuit are the U.S. Open, the British Open, and the PGA Championship.

Tiger's appearance at the Masters caused a stir. No African-American played at the Masters until 1975, and it wasn't until 1990 that the Augusta National Golf Course, where the tournament was played each year, admitted a black member. Tiger acted nonchalant about his appearance there, perhaps because the tournament had scorned black golfers for so many years. Though he tried to downplay his racial background, Tiger had to get used to the fact that it attracted as much attention as his

His best effort. When faced with problems or criticism, Woods has always reacted by focusing on his game.

golf. *GQ* magazine predicted that Tiger Woods's racial heritage, combined with his golf abilities, would enable him to be one of the most influential people of the future.

He began preparing for the Masters after he won the U.S. Amateur. He studied videotapes of previous matches at Augusta National to get an idea of what the course would be like. Once there, Tiger played rounds with some of the world's best golfers, such as Greg Norman and Fred Couples. He made the cut, then came in tied for forty-first place—a less-than-spectacular finish. But his drives of more than 300 yards (274 m) were an indication that Woods would return to the Masters. "I needed binoculars to see where he hit the ball," said the defending Masters champion, Jose Maria Olazabal. Gary Player, another major golf pro, commented at the tournament that "as soon as I saw Tiger Woods swing today, I thought, man, this young guy has got it." Player predicted Woods would experience the same long success enjoyed by Jack Nicklaus and Arnold Palmer. After the tournament, as he often did, Tiger played some exhibition golf at a local public golf course for a mostly African-American crowd.

College Frustration

As much as Tiger liked being at Stanford, he experienced a variety of frustrations when it came to the golf team. For instance, he went through a period of injuries that took him out of some tournaments. Then when he did play, he wasn't consistent. In addition, the National Collegiate Athletic Association (NCAA), the organization that governs college sports, had many rules that Tiger found irritating. But he continued to do well in school, maintaining a B average in his classes as he juggled college and golf. He decided he would try to play more professional matches in 1995 to keep his golf game moving forward.

His first big tournament that year was the U.S. Open, but he injured his wrist early on and withdrew from the tournament. He also played the British Open that summer at the Royal and Ancient Golf Club of St. Andrews, Scotland, where the game of golf began. Tiger was awed by the historic surroundings of "buildings and walls that were built in the 1400s—you don't see that in [Los Angeles]." Though his play was not outstanding (he tied for sixty-eighth place), he did make the cut at this

With Greg Norman. Even as an amateur, Woods shared practice rounds with many established golfers at the Masters.

major tournament, which he hadn't done at the last British Open.

When it was time for the next U.S. Amateur tournament in Newport, Rhode Island, Woods was on a losing streak. He hadn't won a tournament

Back to back. Tiger Woods won his second U.S. Amateur Championship in 1995.

since he played at Shoal Creek ten months earlier. It didn't look like his golf had improved over the year, Woods said, because he was playing in more difficult professional tournaments. His goal now was to win two U.S. Amateurs in a row, something golfers seldom do, and which Jack Nicklaus had never done. At first it didn't look like that would happen. Woods barely made the cut and said he was "extremely disappointed" with his golf up to that point. But he rallied to his goal of winning. Woods and Buddy Marucci, a forty-three-year-old businessman, battled it out for the championship. Their scores remained close but at the par-four eighteenth hole, Woods executed a shot he had been practicing since spring, and with his second shot got the ball close enough to the hole to putt for a birdie—one stroke under par. He'd won his second U.S. Amateur. He also qualified again to enter the 1996 Masters, U.S. Open, and British Open.

Playing with the Pros

By this time, Tiger's racial background had become less of an issue. The new topic of discussion concerning Tiger Woods was: When would he turn pro? Not if, but *when?* Tiger didn't feel ready yet to become a professional though. And he wanted to remain an amateur long enough to win a third consecutive U.S. Amateur, something no one else had achieved.

At his next Masters appearance in spring 1996,

Tiger had a practice round with Jack Nicklaus and Arnold Palmer, which drew a huge crowd. Nicklaus noted the improvement in Tiger's golf game, calling him "the most fundamentally sound golfer I've seen at almost any age." Gary Player was on the course practicing just ahead of Tiger and the two golf veterans. Player told the spectators who watched him practice, "Go look at that fellow playing behind me. That's golf's next superstar." Woods continued seeking information from the pros about different golf courses or how to handle celebrity, and they gave him tips on playing the Augusta National Course. Once again, Woods failed to make the cut at the Masters, but he wasn't discouraged. As Nicklaus told Tiger, it had taken him five tries before he won there. Woods returned to Stanford to finish out the golf season.

Another goal of Tiger's was to win an NCAA championship, which he did as the school year finished up in 1996. But he knew that if he continued playing college golf, his game might suffer. He felt he needed the challenge of professional events to stay motivated. On the other hand, he wasn't sure he was ready to turn pro, and he wanted to play in the upcoming U.S. Amateur. He delayed making any

Crowd pleasers. Many fans watched as Tiger Woods, Arnold Palmer, and Jack Nicklaus practiced at the 1996 Masters.

Tiger Woods: Professional Golfer

decisions about his future until he could see how well he did at the U.S. Open and the British Open during the summer of 1996.

First came the U.S. Open. After the first two days of play, he made the cut with scores of a six-over-par 76, and a one-under-par 69. In the next two days he scored a 77 and a 72, which tied him for eighty-second place.

When he appeared on "The Tonight Show with Jay Leno" after that, Leno held up a picture of baby Tiger swinging a golf club. "You don't see many pros in diapers," Leno remarked.

"I should have had one on at the Open," joked Tiger about coming in eighty-second at the tournament.

He performed better at the British Open. He finished in a tie for twenty-second and was awarded the Silver Medal that goes to the best-scoring amateur. Woods was feeling closer to his goal of readiness for professional golf. His coach Butch Harmon encouraged him in that direction too.

Though Tiger wasn't a pro yet, he was increasingly asked for interviews and autographs. Because he wasn't always sure how to handle that, he scheduled a dinner with Arnold Palmer to seek his advice. Palmer picked up the check for dinner, and suddenly Woods found himself in trouble with the NCAA. Its rules were so strict for college athletes that Tiger was accused of taking an illegal gift, in the form of dinner. He was suspended from college golf for one day and had to repay Palmer the $25. He'd already found it irritating when, due to NCAA regulations, he wasn't allowed to play with certain golf equipment because it wasn't Stanford's usual brand.

Tiger was growing tired of what seemed like too much scrutiny by the NCAA into his golf life. He decided that the incident with Arnold Palmer gave him another good reason to put amateur golf behind him. It was a difficult decision though, because Woods thoroughly enjoyed his classes at Stanford and living in the dormitory with other college students. But there was little to challenge him in college golf anymore. By the summer of 1996, reporters were speculating on his turning pro. Pro golfer Curtis Strange was asked in a television interview about the subject. He thought Tiger should make the move because "You learn how to play golf out here; you don't do it in the amateur ranks." Tiger came to the same conclusion. After a poor performance in the Western Amateur tournament in Michigan, Tiger wasn't discouraged. He believed that he was losing interest in amateur golf. He was ready for the challenges of professional golf. But before he made that announcement, he wanted to be the first man to win three consecutive U.S. Amateurs.

Moving on. When Woods turned pro, he exchanged his Stanford cap for one provided by Nike.

THE BIG STEP: TURNING PRO

Tiger Woods didn't immediately announce his intention to turn pro after he played the U.S. Amateur in 1996. But he didn't need to. It was obvious.

IMG would be representing Tiger's business interests, and they'd hammered out an endorsement contract for Tiger with Nike. Tiger and Earl had flown from Cypress, California, to the U.S. Amateur tournament at Pumpkin Ridge in Oregon. Nike chief Phil Knight drove from the nearby Nike headquarters in Beaverton, Oregon, to watch Tiger play. From there, Nike flew Tiger to

Milwaukee, Wisconsin. Athletes who fly via corporate jet, it's safe to assume, don't expect to return to college sports.

When Tiger arrived in Oregon his immediate goal was to win his third U.S. Amateur. A golfer named Bobby Jones had won five U.S. Amateurs in the 1920s. He retired from golf at age twenty-eight

and was still considered to have been the best American amateur golfer ever. Though he'd remained an amateur, Jones had achieved golf's Grand Slam, meaning he won each of the major tournaments at least once. But Bobby Jones never won three U.S. Amateur tournaments in a row. Tiger wanted to add that achievement to his growing list of "firsts."

The best amateur ever? Bobby Jones won five amateur championships during the 1920s.

Handling All the Attention

Woods may have learned in the past to tune out distractions. But before it even began, this tournament had become a three-ring circus around Tiger Woods. The fact that Phil Knight was at Pumpkin Ridge to watch Tiger play told reporters that Woods would soon be endorsing, or helping to sell, Nike products. An amateur college athlete wouldn't be allowed to do that under NCAA rules. But a professional athlete could. Curious reporters were anxious to break the news of Tiger turning pro. But Woods kept quiet on that subject. There were representatives from other sports-management agencies who vied for Tiger's attention. And his appearance there generated a record number of people attending the Amateur. Because of her height, Kultida couldn't have hoped to see her son play over the heads and shoulders of the crowd there. So she was given special permission to watch her son from inside the ropes that spectators stand behind.

As an amateur, Tiger had learned to juggle golf and schoolwork. He'd never had to hold a job. His parents supported him and his golf expenses. His golf game gave him free entry to a country club where he could practice, and he attended Stanford on a golf scholarship.

But once he decided to turn pro, Tiger would have plenty to think about. At age twenty, he went from being an unemployed college student to pondering what he would do with the $40 million Nike would be paying him over the next five years. Equipment manufacturer Titleist was going to pay him $10 million to use their golf balls and other products.

No doubt he was coaxed to move to Florida by his father or IMG or both. He said he wanted to avoid the high California state income tax, something to which most twenty-year-olds, even those with a lot of money, wouldn't give much thought. So when he turned professional, he made Orlando his home base. Florida has no state income tax and is home to many professional athletes for that reason. Once the Amateur was over, Woods faced pressure to perform well during his first several weeks of professional golf. Otherwise he would be limited in how much he could participate in PGA tournaments in 1997.

That was quite a lot to think about even for an extraordinary young man like Tiger Woods. But he would have to shut it all out and focus on one thing: winning this particular tournament.

Reaching His Goal

Tiger made it look easy as he got off to a strong start. He scored a 69 and a 67 during the first two rounds, the lowest score among all the entrants. In his book about Tiger Woods, John Strege tells the story of how, after making the tournament cut, Tiger made his usual morning stop at McDonald's drive-through

Number three. Woods talked with his mother during the 1996 U.S. Amateur tournament he would eventually win.

window for breakfast. He saw a photo of himself hanging by the window and realized employees there were keeping track of his orders.

He continued to breeze through the next rounds. When he faced seventeen-year-old Charles Howell, Tiger might have been reminded of himself a few years earlier. He also faced his Stanford golf team-mate and friend Joel Kribel. In the past they liked to challenge each other to taco-eating contests at Taco Bell. But on the golf course, Tiger was all business and defeated Kribel. As Tiger made his way through the tournament, the "pro" rumors gathered momentum. But Tiger remained focused on his goal of winning.

In the final round, Tiger faced another college student, Steve Scott from the University of Florida. Woods didn't make his usual strong charge into the match. In fact, he double-bogeyed at the second hole, and hit two shots into the water at the fifth hole. By the end of the first nine holes, Woods was five strokes behind, and Steve Scott probably thought he had a chance at the championship. As they broke for lunch, Tiger gave Butch Harmon a call to talk about the match, and Harmon suggested Tiger adjust his posture for his swing and his putt.

As he returned to play, Tiger was in a situation that might have rattled a player as young as he was. He faced the pressure of professional golf looming ahead of him, crowds of people there to watch him, and being five strokes behind in a golf tournament that he very much wanted to win. But then Tiger did what he does best—he willed himself to play unbeatable golf. As the play wore on in the afternoon, Scott found himself leading by only one stroke. At the seventeenth hole, Tiger needed to make a 30-foot (9-m) putt—and he did. Even he said the shot seemed "unbelievable." The score was tied, and play extended to an extra hole. Scott might have won with an 18-foot (5.5-m) birdie putt, but he missed, and the match went to another extra hole.

Woods teed off the ball to land within 7 feet (2 m) of the hole, then failed to putt for a birdie. But he didn't need to. Scott got into trouble by hitting the ball into the rough, or tall grass, then missed his putt after getting the ball back onto the green. It was Tiger's match. "Against Tiger Woods, no lead is secure," said Steve Scott after the match. "He's just so difficult to beat." Another first for Tiger: his mother was there to give him a congratulatory hug

Tiger Woods: Professional Golfer

this time. She wanted to be there since she hadn't attended his previous amateur tournaments.

A Big Change

Tired as he was, Tiger had little time to rest. He spent a quiet evening playing cards with friend Byron Bell. Then, two days after winning his third U.S. Amateur, he made the announcement that the golf world had been awaiting. "As of now, I am a professional golfer," he announced in a news release. He asked reporters to allow him "to practice without distraction today." When he announced his decision personally before reporters, he greeted them with "Hello, World." The simple phrase was actually a slogan crafted for Tiger Woods by Nike. It would be part of Nike's multi-million-dollar advertising campaign. Beginning right then, Tiger has been decked out in Nike clothing from head to toe.

Tiger flew to Milwaukee in Nike's corporate jet to play in the Greater Milwaukee Open, a professional event. He decided to start his pro career in smaller events like that one and the Quad City Classic in Illinois. Woods wanted to avoid the heaviest competition while he tried to earn enough tournament

"Hello, World." With support from his father, Tiger Woods announced his entrance into professional golf.

money to qualify for the 1997 PGA Tour membership. If he finished in the top 125 money earners before the end of the year, he would make it.

At the Milwaukee Open, Woods came in tied for sixtieth place. He picked up his first paycheck for playing golf—$2,544. Though his professional debut wasn't spectacular, he thrilled spectators with a hole-in-one on his last day, and he gave the ball to a fan. Between his U.S. Amateur win and his first game as a pro, Woods "was on television so much it seemed as though he had his own show," wrote a *Los Angeles Times* reporter.

His next tournament was an improvement. He played the Bell Canadian Open and came in eleventh, earning $37,500, putting his total at just over $40,000. He still had six weeks and five PGA tournaments left to play before the season ended.

Publicity—and More Publicity

In the meantime, Woods got his first taste of bad public relations. Nike didn't waste any time using Woods in its advertising, and a large ad appeared in *The Wall Street Journal* and on television. "There are still golf courses in the United States that I cannot play because of the color of my skin," Woods claimed in the ads. "Are you ready for me?" The controversial language of the ad was typical for Nike, but it seemed out of character for Tiger Woods.

As many in the media pointed out, Tiger Woods could probably play golf anywhere he wanted to, as popular as he was. "Just where *couldn't* he play?" one reporter asked Nike. Well, nowhere, actually, Nike admitted. The ad, said a Nike spokesperson, was simply implying that there was still racism in golf in general. But using Tiger Woods for that message didn't go over well because Tiger had spent years downplaying his racial heritage. And just as he was being welcomed into professional golf, he was giving it a slam. Some pro golfers already resented him for earning so much money with endorsements at such a young age. Other professionals who'd been supportive of him were not impressed. Jim Thorpe, another African-American on the PGA Tour, thought Nike and Tiger should have gone for a "more positive message." Almost as quickly as they came out with it, Nike stopped using the ad.

In spite of the negative publicity, however, Tiger stayed on track with his golf. After placing eleventh in Canada, Woods went to Illinois to play in the

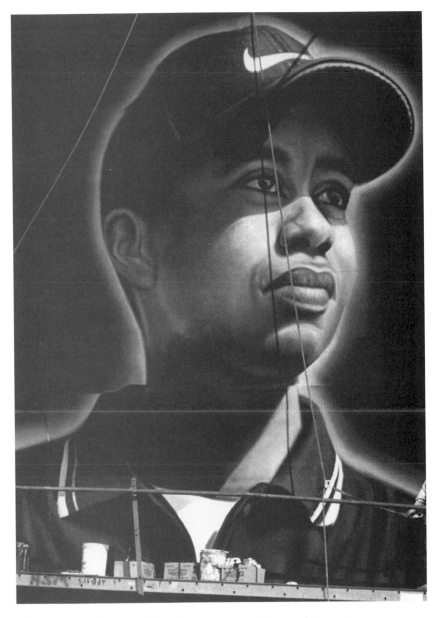

The face of Nike. Woods has become one of the world's most recognized athletes.

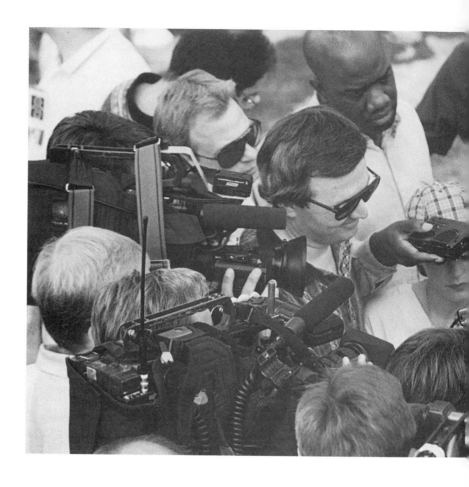

Quad City Classic. It was occurring at the same time as the Presidents Cup tournament outside Washington, D.C., which was considered a more important tournament. At one point Woods was leading by one stroke and some reporters left the Presidents Cup match to watch Woods play in Coal Valley, Illinois. This time, Tiger tied for fifth place, earning $42,150.

Cameras and questions. The media attention Woods received in 1996 was exciting but overwhelming.

He moved up another notch in his next tournament—the Buick Challenge Open in Endicott, New York—where he tied for third. In four weeks of professional play and four tournaments, he'd earned more than $140,000 and was then 128th on the PGA earnings list. There was still much more work for Tiger Woods to do.

By now, Woods was exhausted. He'd won the U.S. Amateur, which was immediately followed by four more tournaments. He'd weathered the Nike ad controversy and the media whirlwind over joining the professional ranks of golf. His next stop was Georgia to play the Buick Challenge. He went through one practice round and declared himself too tired to continue play in the tournament. Also, an award dinner in Pine Mountain, Georgia, was scheduled in his honor. The Fred Haskins Award honors the top college golfer each year and, several months earlier, Woods had committed to being there. Although 200 people had bought tickets to attend, Woods canceled his appearance there too. He soon received another lesson in bad public relations.

The criticism he received for bowing out of the tournament and the dinner came from not just the media, but from his fellow golfers as well. None came to his defense. "How quickly he forgot" that the Buick Challenge organizers gave Woods a sponsors' exemption to play in the tournament to help him earn enough money to play the PGA Tour in 1997, said his usual supporter, Curtis Strange.

"Everybody has been telling him how great he is. I guess he's starting to believe it," said Davis Love III.

Even his friend and advisor Arnold Palmer admitted that, "Tiger should have played. He should have gone to the dinner." Woods, now a professional golfer, was being held to higher standards.

In his book about Tiger Woods, sportswriter John Feinstein was critical of the way Woods's early professional career was managed by his father Earl Woods and IMG. "Someone in the group that was making itself rich off Woods . . . should have sat him down" and at least insist that he attend the dinner, Feinstein wrote.

Tiger admitted he made a mistake in canceling his participation in the tournament and the dinner. He wrote letters of apology to every person who bought a ticket for the dinner and he paid the cost of the dinner—$30,000—to its organizers. In a column that appeared in *Golf World* magazine, he said that though he was very tired by the time he got to Georgia, "what I did was wrong." Woods did eventually appear at the Fred Haskins Award dinner when it was rescheduled.

Facing Challenges

At his next tournament, the Las Vegas Invitational, Woods found a way to rebound from his recent negative publicity. It was an important tournament, with all the major golf players attending. At this five-round event (instead of the usual four), Woods shot a 70 his first day, which put him behind. Though he lowered his score in the next three days' rounds, he still trailed the lead by four strokes in the fifth round. But by the eighteenth hole, Woods and Davis Love III were tied for first place. On the tie-breaking hole, Love missed his par putt, and Woods won his first professional tournament. His earnings from Las Vegas put him well into PGA Tour play for the next two years.

Woods was disappointed with his play at his next tournament, the Texas Open in San Antonio, where he came in third. But the crowds who came to see him were so big that parking space ran out, and people came to the tournament in shuttle buses. Then, as he arrived in his new hometown of Orlando for

Joy and relief. Woods was thrilled to win the 1996 Las Vegas Invitational, his first professional victory.

his last PGA tournament of the year, Woods tried to shake off a virus he'd picked up. He had a sore throat, felt dizzy, and said that his congested head "might burst." Woods's play for round one was a 69, and as in Las Vegas, he was several strokes behind the lead. "Pop, I'm going to shoot a 63 tomorrow," Tiger told his father, and he made good on that promise. He shot a 69 for the third round and was closing in on the lead. For his final round, Kultida phoned to remind him to wear red, his lucky color. Tiger was paired with the late Payne Stewart, who'd been a winner at the U.S. Open and the PGA Championship. Their play was neck and neck, but Tiger won by a stroke—his second PGA Tour win. He ended the year as twenty-fourth on the PGA earnings list.

Late in October, after playing just seven tournaments, Tiger made it to the Tour Championship in Tulsa, Oklahoma (a different event from the PGA Championship held each August). There, in the middle of the tournament, Earl Woods had a heart attack and spent the night in a Tulsa hospital with Tiger by his side. Earl's condition improved, and Tiger returned to the golf course the next day. But his mind wasn't on golf. He ended up tied for twenty-first place in the tournament and returned to the hospital to be with his father, who was diagnosed with coronary blockage and pneumonia. For once, golf was the last thing on Tiger's mind.

Nevertheless, it had been quite a year. He had charged into professional golf, winning more than $750,000 in just a couple of months, a stunning debut for a twenty-year-old. Woods was also the object of constant requests for interviews, television appearances, and endorsements. He wasn't just a golfer; he was a phenomenon—a new superstar in sports. And he was just getting started.

Breaking the records. When Woods won the 1997 Masters, he became the tournament's youngest champion.

CHASING THE TIGER

Since 1997, the game of golf has been redefined. It now involves chasing a Tiger. So far, no one has been able to catch him.

Tiger Woods put on quite a show during his first eight months of professional golf. In just a couple of months of play, he had made $98,824, the best tournament earnings average on the PGA Tour by the end of 1996. *Sports Illustrated* magazine named him Sportsman of the Year. The magazine predicted that in spite of his youth and the pressure of being a superstar, he had staying power. So far, that assertion has proven correct.

The Green Jacket

Woods won the Mercedes Championships, his first tournament of 1997, before his father's continuing health problems slowed Tiger's game down. Earl Woods had heart-bypass surgery, and Tiger's play showed his worry. But then came the Masters Tournament in April 1997, and the Tiger-chasing safari began.

After the first nine holes of play on Thursday in the Augusta, Georgia, tournament, it looked as though it could be anyone's game. Tiger himself shot a 40. Then he dug in and made his score for the next nine holes a 30, for a total of 70. That same day, three-time Masters champion Nick Faldo hit a 75; Davis Love finished the day with 72. Most of the players were above 70. By the thirteenth hole on Friday, everyone trailed Woods. Golfer Colin Montgomerie noted that there still were plenty of holes to play and those with more tournament experience could catch up to Woods. But that never happened. By the end of Saturday, Montgomerie admitted, "We're all human. And there's no way it's humanly possible for anyone to catch him tomorrow."

When the tournament ended on Sunday, Woods won by a twelve-stroke lead, the largest ever in the tournament's history. He was also the youngest winner ever—and the first non-white winner. When Woods was awarded the winner's green jacket, he received a standing ovation from his peers. His total score over the tournament's four days had been 270, one stroke better than Jack Nicklaus's best-ever Masters score of 271. Nicklaus predicted that Woods would win as many Masters tournaments as Nicklaus and Arnold Palmer combined—eleven.

Perfecting His Swing

But rather than cruise on his victory—and his number-one status—Woods thought he could do better. After he watched videotapes of his Masters play, he decided that his swing wasn't what it should be. His swing's timing was good, he knew, but he thought the position of his hips and wrist needed improvement, and his arms needed strengthening. The outcome, he was confident, would give him better control over his long shots and consistently better shots. So he called in Butch Harmon to help him

Perfect fit. Nick Faldo, the 1996 Masters champion, helped Woods put on the winning green jacket.

redo his swing. Woods knew it wouldn't happen overnight but would take at least several months.

In fact, after his extraordinary eight-month start, Woods would win only one PGA Tour event in the next year and a half. Fans and the media sometimes expressed disappointment in his play, which he found frustrating. "Winning is not always the barometer of getting better," he said during that time. By 1999, David Duval had replaced Woods as the game's best player.

But that May, as he practiced for the upcoming Byron Nelson Classic in Dallas, Texas, Woods realized his new swing had arrived. "I think I'm back," he told Harmon in a phone call. At the Nelson tournament, he started strong with scores of 61 and 67, but couldn't maintain that. However, his swing soon came through for him when he won a tournament in Heidelberg, Germany. Then, in June, he played the Memorial Tournament at Jack Nicklaus's Muirfield Village Golf Club in Dublin, Ohio. He defeated Vijay Singh by two strokes. A very satisfied Tiger Woods accepted the winner's crystal trophy from Nicklaus. When he won at the Western Open in Illinois later that summer, his rank in golf went back to number one.

A special victory. Woods was honored to receive the Memorial Tournament trophy from Jack Nicklaus.

His Second Major

Showing that his new swing wasn't a fluke, Tiger captured his second major title by winning the PGA Championship in August. He won five of the PGA's next six tour events, the longest winning streak in forty-six years. As he came back in 1999 with his best game yet, other players were realizing that golf would be different now. "We've got to keep stepping it up a notch," said Davis Love III of his and others' play. "But while we've been saying that, he's stepped it up another notch." Woods's total earnings for the 1999 golf season, more than $6 million, broke another record. The previous record had been David Duval's $2.6 million. As the season came to an end, Woods's fellow golfers voted him PGA Tour Player of the Year.

The comparisons with Nicklaus remained frequent: Nicklaus had won three major titles by age twenty-three, while Woods gathered his second at that age. But he had taken "time off" to work on his swing. Besides, Nicklaus said, "the competition is so much keener now" than it had been in his glory days. Nicklaus believed that Woods's play of 1999 had surpassed any of Nicklaus's best years. But Nicklaus had yet to see 2000.

Skill and scenery. Woods captured his third major title at the 2000 U.S. Open in Pebble Beach.

The U.S. Open

June 2000, Pebble Beach, California: Sportswriters had to think of more ways to say "amazing" as they watched Tiger Woods win his first U.S. Open. He set the record for a winning margin—fifteen strokes—in

any major championship. He was now considered the best driver (or long-range hitter), the best chipper, and the best putter in golf. The challenging course by the Pacific Ocean had heavy areas of "rough," winds off the ocean, and hard putting greens that gave golf balls plenty of unwanted bounce and roll.

While Woods breezed through it, the other players battled it out for second place (Ernie Els of South Africa and Miguel Angel Jimenez of Spain tied for second). After his performance there, sportswriters seemed to agree, it was no use comparing Woods to anyone, today or in history, including greats like Jack Nicklaus or Bobby Jones.

The British Open

One month later at St. Andrews, Woods captured his career Grand Slam win—he'd now won the Masters, the U.S. Open, the British Open, and the PGA Championship, only the fifth golfer to do so. At age twenty-four, he was two years younger than Nicklaus when he claimed his Grand Slam title.

During one round, his partner, David Toms, was amazed with Woods's ability to focus on his play. "I have never seen so many people on a golf course," Toms said. "A lot of those people are screaming at him, sometimes when he's standing over a shot. It is awesome to watch." Another record set at the British Open that year was the number of people in attendance— 230,000. While his opponents were digging out of the course's 112 bunkers, Woods's golf balls never veered from the fairway in 72 holes of golf. He shot rounds of 67, 66, 67, and 69. His total score of 269 set a record for the most strokes under par—nineteen—at the British Open. After him were Els again and Thomas Bjorn, who both came in eight strokes behind Woods. Tiger took home the tournament's trophy, a silver claret jug. "It's the ultimate. This is the home of golf. This is where you always want to win," Woods said of his victory there. "To have a chance to complete the [Grand] Slam at St. Andrews is pretty special."

His Second PGA Championship

In August, the golf world turned to its next major tournament, the PGA Championship at Valhalla Golf Club in Louisville, Kentucky. Yes, Woods won, but this time it was a real contest. In the final round, the championship was within reach for both Woods and another former Southern California junior golf star, thirty-one-year-old Bob May. Woods and May had grown up in neighborhoods twenty minutes away from each other. Woods had kept tabs on May's impressive achievements when they were both junior golfers. May spent several years playing golf in European tournaments, but sud-

Tough opponent. Bob May found himself in a playoff with Woods for the 2000 PGA Championship.

denly he was giving Tiger Woods a run for the PGA Championship.

Woods was behind by two strokes early in the final round of play. He got down to business and played the next twelve holes at seven shots under par. They started the back nine holes at a tie, trading off the lead as they went along. The round went into a three-hole playoff, a new rule in PGA events. Woods hit a birdie and made par on the last two shots. May hit a drive into thick rough on the last playoff hole, which sank his chance of besting Woods. Tiger enjoyed his intense duel with Bob May. In fact, he called it his toughest match ever. "It was an incredible battle. We never backed off," Tiger said. "Birdie for birdie, shot for shot, that's as good as it gets."

Breaking Records

Tiger Woods became only the second player, after Ben Hogan in 1953, to win three major tournaments in one season. As golf seasons are measured, great ones have included Hogan's three-major winner in 1953, Bobby Jones' Grand Slam in 1930, and Byron Nelson's 1945 eighteen-tournament win, eleven of which were in a row. But Woods's 2000 season is now considered the one to beat. He had ten wins by early December, but the records he set at the major tournaments will likely stand for quite some time. That season, his scoring average for a round of golf was the lowest in golf history as well: 67.79. That's the lowest average since Sam Snead averaged 69.23 in 1950.

Another legend. Ben Hogan was the first player to win three major tournaments in one season.

Tom Watson, who won the U.S. Open in 1982, summed it up for other golfers. He said that "Tiger has raised the bar, and it seems that he's the only guy who can jump over that bar."

Giving back. Through his clinics and the Tiger Woods Foundation, Woods wants to bring golf to everyone.

WHO IS TIGER? **7**

Golf skills always seemed to develop naturally for Tiger Woods, especially since he loved to work at it. Unless he can recall being a newborn, he wouldn't remember a time when he wasn't swinging a golf club.

What's been more difficult for him has been learning to live under an intense spotlight. He complained once to Arnold Palmer that between fans and reporters, he couldn't be a normal twenty-one-year-old. Palmer told him, "Tiger, normal twenty-one-year-olds don't have $50 million in the bank."

An Unusual Life

Tiger has never lived what most kids would consider a "normal" life. He put all his energy into one sport and began flying around the country to tournaments before he was a teenager. There wasn't much time for socializing in high school, and he never spent a summer sacking groceries or cutting lawns to earn spending money.

His unusual childhood, he discovered, was nothing compared to hearing thousands of fans screaming his name at tournaments. The fame, the millions of dollars, the comparisons to other sports superstars such as Michael Jordan changed his life even more. And people expect more from a highly paid athlete than just a winning record. Turning pro, Woods realized, meant reading about his mistakes in the newspaper or hearing about them on the news.

The Public Eye

He didn't expect so much criticism after he canceled his appearances at the golf tournament and the awards dinner in Georgia in 1996, for example. He also received bad press when he declined an invitation from President Bill Clinton to appear with Clinton and the widow of black baseball pioneer Jackie Robinson at a special ceremony honoring Robinson. Just as he tries to learn from mistakes he makes in his golf game, Tiger tries to learn from the mistakes he makes off the course as well. And knowing he won't please everyone, he's come to realize that it's important "to just be yourself." But who is that person?

Important Relationships

Many of Tiger's "fans" aren't strangers who watch him play golf on television. They're people who've known him for years. "I love Tiger," says Hal Sutton, another golf pro. "He's considerate when I play with him. He's just a great guy."

Tiger is known for giving opponents a thumbs-up sign when they make a good shot. "He is a tremendously well-balanced young man. He is a gracious loser. . . . He will be a great influence on generations of people throughout the world," says golf veteran Gary Player.

But in spite of such predictions, Woods still sees himself as a normal young man. He has a girlfriend now, and "I do everything the same" as other twenty-somethings, such as going to movies or restaurants, he told an interviewer after he won his fifth major tournament in the summer of 2000. He's learned to be more private with reporters but still remains polite.

Woods has made more friends among other PGA Tour golfers too. At first, surrounded by security guards who even intimidated the other golfers, Woods spent little time with his fellow pros. Today, "he's more open and accepting. I'm proud of him as a friend for the way he's conducted himself off the course," said tour golfer Mark O'Meara.

When not playing golf, Tiger enjoys video games and watches sports with friends. He's building a new home in Orlando, where he's become close to fellow sports celebrities Ken Griffey, Jr., and Michael Jordan. He tried salmon fishing in Ireland with O'Meara the week before the British Open, and he then went scuba diving in the Bahamas after his St. Andrews victory. He still participates in golf clinics for disadvantaged youth. At one clinic he held in New Orleans, Woods confided to the kids that he needed special reading classes when he was a boy to help him overcome a speech problem.

Building friendships. Woods has established important relationships with other golfers including Mark O'Meara.

What the Future May Hold

After his spectacular wins in 2000, some people have questioned whether or not Woods can maintain his intense interest in golf. In 1998, while he was working on a new swing, he said in an interview, "I love playing golf more than I ever have." But at that point, he was still amid the challenge of perfecting his play.

In the past, his golf suffered when he became bored at a certain level. He knew, for example, when his junior golf days had come to an end, just as he knew when it was time to move past amateur and college golf. Now, as he's found his ultimate game and when he wins tournaments by a dozen or more strokes, will his interest begin to wane again? "He has to have challengers for the whole thing to be right," Jack Nicklaus told reporters after Woods won the British Open in 2000. But challengers to Woods seemed to have "thrown up the white flag and surrendered," Nicklaus said.

As 2001 began, Tiger Woods remained a strong force on the golf course. But in many PGA tournaments, other players proved they could hold their own again the talented Tiger after all. No doubt, he

A gentleman and a champ. Tiger Woods seems to have a bright future both on and off the golf course.

will continue to dominate play, but is he invincible? Only time will tell.

In the meantime, his popularity continues to grow. In January 2001, Nike struck a deal with Nordstrom department stores to carry a line of Tiger Woods clothing. Before this deal, Tiger's shirts, vests, and slacks had been available at resorts only. It seems that Tiger's name has become a huge part of our modern culture.

In the future, Tiger may seek out challenges off the golf course. He has promised his parents that he will finish his college degree someday. And his Tiger Woods Foundation has the potential to make a difference in the lives of young people everywhere. Whatever his future holds, Woods wants to keep on growing. "Each year I've learned that much more about myself. I guarantee I'll be a totally different person next year from who I am now." He's not worried about being a superhero. "I just want to be me. Tiger Woods."

TIMELINE

1975 Eldrick (Tiger) Woods born on December 30 in Cypress, California, to Earl and Kultida Woods

1976 Takes first swing with a golf club

1977 Plays first hole of golf

1978 First appears on TV news and "The Mike Douglas Show"

1980 Begins playing with teaching pro Rudy Duran

1981 Appears on TV show "That's Incredible"

1982 Plays with golf-great Sam Snead and enters first international tournament

1986 Cuts out Jack Nicklaus's list of lifetime achievements for future comparison; begins working with teaching pro John Anselmo

1987 Goes undefeated, winning thirty junior tournaments

1989 Appears on "Today Show," "Good Morning, America," ESPN, and network television news shows; plays in tournament in Texarkana, Texas, against several professionals and beats eight of them; first hears from Stanford's golf coach Wally Goodwin

1991 As high school freshman is top U.S. junior player; wins first Junior Amateur championship

1992	Wins second Junior Amateur; gains the attention of IMG; plays in PGA Tour's L.A. Open
1993	Wins third Junior Amateur Championship
1994	Wins first U.S. Amateur; enters Stanford University on golf scholarship; wins tournament at Shoal Creek Country Club in Birmingham, Alabama
1995	Wins second U.S. Amateur; returns to Stanford for sophomore year; wins NCAA Championship in golf
1996	Wins third consecutive U.S. Amateur, first player to do so; announces decision to become professional golfer; wins two events and earns enough money from tournaments to qualify for 1997 and 1998 PGA Tour; establishes Tiger Woods Foundation; is named Sportsman of the Year by *Sports Illustrated*
1997	Wins Masters Tournament in April, the youngest winner in history by the largest margin ever
1998	While working on swing, finishes in top ten in thirteen out of twenty tournaments
1999	Wins eight PGA events, including his second major tournament, the PGA Championship; sets record for golf earnings in one season ($6.6 million); ranks as world's top golfer
2000	Maintains golf ranking by winning the U.S. Open in June and the British Open in July, becoming the fifth and youngest golfer to achieve the Grand Slam in golf; wins second PGA Championship, bringing total career earnings to more than $19 million

A GLOSSARY OF GOLF TERMS

Back nine   The last nine holes of an eighteen-hole golf course

Birdie   One stroke under par

Bogey   One stroke over par

Bunker   A place on the golf course, near where a shot may end, that is filled by sand or grass and is designed to obstruct play

Chip   A shot that hits the ball high enough into the air to land on the green and roll toward the hole

Double-bogey   Two strokes over par

Drive   A shot that hits the ball a long distance—often from the tee to the fairway

Fairway   The closely mowed area of grass between the tee and the green

Hole-in-one   A shot that hits the ball from the tee to the hole in just one stroke

Par   The number of shots it should take a good golfer per hole or round

Putt   A shot on the green that hits the golf ball near the hole

Putting green   The area of short grass around the hole

Rough   The high grass next to the fairway and green

Round   Eighteen holes of golf

Sudden-death playoff   The extra holes played after a tie. The first player to win a hole wins the match.

HOW TO
BECOME AN
ATHLETE

The Job

Amateur athletes play or compete for titles or trophies, but not for money. Professional athletes in sports, such as tennis, figure-skating, golf, running, or boxing, compete for money and prizes.

In tennis and boxing, an athlete may compete against one person. In some sports, such as figure skating, golf, and cycling, an athlete may compete against six to thirty people. In certain individual events, such as the New York Marathon, tens of thousands of runners may compete.

The winners of individual sports are evaluated differently. For example, the winner of a foot race is the one who crosses the finish line first. In tennis the winner is the player who wins the most games in a given number of sets. In boxing and figure skating, a panel of judges chooses the winners. Competitions are organized by groups who promote the sport. In a professional sport, different levels of competition are based on age, ability, and gender. There are often different designations and events within one sport. Tennis, for example, consists of doubles and singles, while track and field contains many different events.

Athletes train year-round. Some work on their own. Others work with a coach, friend, parent, or trainer. In addition to stretching and exercising specific muscles, athletes develop eating and sleeping habits that help them stay in top condition throughout the year. Most professional athletes train all year. They vary the type and duration of their workouts to develop strength, flexibility, and speed. They also work on technique and control. Often, an athlete's training focuses on specific details of the game or program. For example, figure skaters may concentrate on jumps, turns, and hand movements. Similarly, sprinters vary their workouts to include some distance work, some sprints, weight training, and maybe some mental exercises to build control and focus while in the starter's blocks. Tennis players spend hours practicing particular shots.

Requirements

High School A high-school diploma provides the basic skills needed to become a professional athlete. Business and mathematics classes teach you how to manage money wisely. Speech classes help you become a better communicator. Physical-education classes help build strength, agility, and competitive spirit. You should, of course, participate in every organized sport that interests you.

In some individual sports, such as tennis and gymnastics, some competitors are high-school students.

Teenagers in this situation often have private coaches. Many practice before and after school, while others are home-schooled as they travel to competitions.

Postsecondary There are no formal education requirements for sports, but certain opportunities are available only to students in four-year colleges and universities. Many athletes develop their skills in college-level competitions. Outstanding ability in athletics enables many students to obtain a college education. An education is always a wise investment.

Other Requirements So much competition exists among athletes in any given sport that talent alone is not the primary requirement. Perseverance, hard work, ambition, and courage are all essential qualities for the individual who dreams of becoming a professional athlete. "If you want to be a pro, there's no halfway. There's no three-quarters way," says Eric Roller, a former professional tennis player. Other requirements vary according to the sport. Jockeys, for example, are usually small-boned men and women.

Exploring

If you are interested in pursuing a career in professional sports, you should start participating in that sport as much and as early as possible. An individual may be too old at fifteen to realistically begin pursuing a professional career in some sports. By playing the sport and by talking to coaches, trainers, and athletes in the field, you can learn whether you like the sport enough to make it a career and whether you have enough talent. You can also learn a lot about the sport. You can contact professional organizations and associations for information on how to best prepare for a career in a particular sport. Some specialized training programs are available. The best way to find out about them is to get in touch with the organizations that promote the sport.

Employers

Professional athletes in individual sports do not work for employers. They choose the competitions or tournaments they wish to enter. For example, a professional runner may choose to run in the Boston Marathon and then travel to Atlanta for the Peachtree Road Race.

Starting Out

Professional athletes must meet the requirements established by the groups that organize their sport. Sometimes this means meeting a physical standard, such as age, height, or weight, and sometimes it means participating in a certain number of competitions. Professional organizations usually arrange it so that athletes can build up their skills by taking part in lower-level competitions. College sports are an excellent way to improve one's skills while pursuing an education.

Advancement

Professional athletes get ahead in their sport by working and practicing hard, and by winning. Professional athletes usually have agents who make deals for them, such as which team they will play for and how much they will be paid. These agents may also be involved with the athlete's commercial endorsements, taxes, and financial investments.

A college education can prepare all athletes for the day when their bodies can no longer compete at the top level. Every athlete should be prepared to move into another career.

Earnings

Salaries, cash prizes, and commercial endorsements vary from sport to sport. A lot depends on the popularity of the sport and its ability to attract fans. Still other sports, like boxing, depend on the skill of the fight's promoters to create interest in the fight. An elite professional tennis player who wins Wimbledon, for example, usually earns more than half a million dollars in a matter of two weeks. Add to that the incredible sums a Wimbledon-champion can make in endorsements and the tennis star is earning more than one million dollars a year. This scenario is misleading, however; to begin with, top athletes usually cannot perform at such a level for very long, which is why a good accountant and investment counselor comes in handy. Second, for every top athlete who earns millions of dollars in a year, there are hundreds of professional athletes who earn less than $40,000. The stakes are incredibly high, the competition fierce.

The financial success of an athlete may depend greatly on the individual's character or personality. An athlete who has a nasty temper or is known to behave badly may be able to win games but may not be able to cash in on the commercial endorsements. Advertisers are careful about whom they choose to endorse products. Some athletes have lost million-dollar accounts because of bad behavior on or off the field.

Many athletes go into some area of coaching, sports

administration, management, or broadcasting. The professional athlete's insight can be a great asset in these careers. Some athletes simultaneously pursue interests completely unrelated to their sport, such as education, business, social welfare, or the arts. Many enjoy coaching young people or volunteering with local school teams.

Work Environment

Athletes compete in many kinds of conditions. Track-and-field athletes often compete in hot or rainy conditions, but officials can call off the meet or postpone competition until better weather at any point. Indoor events are less subject to cancellation. An athlete may withdraw from competition if he or she is injured or ill. However, nerves and fear are not good reasons to quit a competition. Part of climbing up the ranks is learning to cope with such feelings. Some athletes actually thrive on the nervous tension.

The expenses of a sport can also be overwhelming. In addition to specialized equipment and clothing, the athlete must pay for a coach, travel expenses, competition fees, and, depending on the sport, time at the gym. Tennis, golf, figure skating, and skiing are among the most expensive sports. And even after all the hard work, practice, and financial sacrifice, making big money is a rarity.

Outlook

On the whole, the outlook for the field of professional sports is healthy, but the number of jobs will not increase dramatically. Some sports, however, may become more popular, which will mean greater opportunities for higher salaries, cash prizes, and commercial endorsements.

TO LEARN MORE ABOUT ATHLETES

Books

Coffey, Wayne. *Carl Lewis: The Triumph of Discipline*. Woodbridge, Conn.: Blackbirch Press, 1992.

Freedman, Russell. *Babe Didrikson Zaharias*. New York: Clarion, 1999.

Krull, Kathleen. *Lives of the Athletes : Thrills, Spills (And What the Neighbors Thought)*. New York: Harcourt Brace, 1997.

Rudeen, Kenneth. *Jackie Robinson*. New York: HarperTrophy, 1996.

Stewart, Mark. *Florence Griffith-Joyner*. Danbury, Conn.: Children's Press, 1997.

Stewart, Mark. *Tiger Woods: Driving Force*. Danbury, Conn.: Children's Press, 1998.

Updyke, Rosemary Kissinger. *Jim Thorpe, the Legend Remembered*. New York: Pelican, 1997.

Websites
Sports Illustrated for Kids
http://www.sikids.com/
An on-line magazine providing news about current athletes and sports

United States Olympic Committee
http://www.olympic-usa.org/
Official site of this committee headquartered in Colorado Springs

USA Track & Field
http://www.usatf.org/
A resource for information about current athletes as well as members of the hall of fame, plus current news and membership

Women in Sports
http://www.makeithappen.com/wis/index.html
Provides information about and links to women in all kinds of sports

Where to Write
Young people who are interested in becoming professional athletes should contact the professional organizations for the sport in which they would like to compete, such as the U.S. Tennis Association, the Professional Golfer's Association, or the National Bowling Association. Ask for information on requirements, training centers, coaches, and so on.

Amateur Athletic Union
c/o The Walt Disney World Resort
P.O. Box 10000
Lake Buena Vista, FL 32830-1000
http://www.aausports.org/
For a free brochure and information on the Junior Olympics and more

American Alliance for Health, Physical Education, Recreation, and Dance
1900 Association Drive
Reston, VA 20191
http://www.aahperd.org/
For additional information on athletics

TO LEARN MORE ABOUT TIGER WOODS

Books

Christopher, Matt. *On the Course with . . . Tiger Woods*. Boston: Little, Brown, 1998.

Durbin, William. *Tiger Woods: Golf Legends*. Broomall, Penn.: Chelsea House, 1998.

Gutman, Bill. *Tiger Woods: Golf's Shining Young Star*. Brookfield, Conn.: Millbrook Press, 1998.

Joseph, Paul. *Tiger Woods*. Edina, Minn.: Abdo & Daughters, 1998.

Rambeck, Richard. *Tiger Woods*. Chanhassen, Minn.: Child's World,1999.

Savage, Jeff. *Tiger Woods: King of the Course*. Minneapolis: Lerner, 1998.

Stewart, Mark. *Tiger Woods: Driving Force*. Sports Star. Danbury, Conn.: Children's Press, 1998.

Websites
Club Tiger
http://www.clubtiger.com
For details about the Tiger Woods fan club

Golf Online
http://www.golfonline.com/
Information about various golfers plus news about the PGA tour

PGATOUR.com
http://golfweb.com/
To track the success of Tiger Woods and other golfers on the PGA tour

Tiger Woods
http://www.tigerwoods.com/
Biographical information, up-to-date news items, and details about the Tiger Woods Foundation

Interesting Places to Visit
Pebble Beach Golf Links
17 Mile Drive
Pebble Beach, California 93953
831/624-3811
To see one of the world's best courses, the site of Tiger's 2000 U.S. Open win

USGA Golf House and Museum
Liberty Corner Road
Far Hills, New Jersey 07931
908/234-2300
A large public collection of vintage golf memorabilia

World Golf Hall of Fame
World Golf Village
21 World Golf Place
St. Augustine, Florida 32092
904/940-4000
To learn all about the game and its great players

INDEX

Page numbers in *italics* indicate illustrations.

Presidents Cup tournament, 76–77

Quad City Classic, 71, 76

racism, 23, 35–36, 47–48, 50, 55, 73–74
Reed, Steward, 25
Robinson, Jackie, 103
Roller, Eric, 115
Royal and Ancient Gold Club, 53

Scott, Steve, 69, 70
Singh, Vijay, 89
Snead, Sam, 25, *26*, 27, 97
Sports Illustrated Sportsman of the Year award, 85
Stanford University, 32–33, 42, 44 45, 53
Strange, Curtis, 60, 79
Strege, John, 37, 68
Sutton, Hal, 103

Texas Open, 80
"That's Incredible" television show, 22
Thompson, Hall, 47
Tiger Woods Foundation, *100*, 108
Titleist, 67
Toms, David, 94
Tour Championship, 82

U.S. Amateur Tournament, 30, 33, *43*, 50, 54, 56, 59, 63–64, 71, 78
U.S. Golf Association (USGA), 30
U.S. Navy golf course, 20
U.S. Open, 53–54, 59, 92–94, *92–93*

Valhalla Golf Club, 95

Watson, Tom, 99
Western Amateur tournament, 42, 61
Western Open, 89
Woods, Earl (father), 10, 15, 16, 18–20, *19*, 25, 29–30, 42, 63, *72*, 79, 82–83, *84*, 86
Woods, Elrick "Tiger," *8, 12, 14, 24, 28, 34, 38–39, 41, 43, 46, 49, 52, 54–55, 57, 62, 72, 76–77, 81, 88, 90, 93, 96, 100, 105, 107*
birth of, 18
childhood of, 10, *14*, 19–23, *19*, 27, 29, *34*
education of, 22–23, 35–36, 40, 45, 47, 53, 60
Woods, Kultida (mother), 15–16, *17*, 18, 20–21, 23, 25, 30, 66, *68*, 70–71, 82

ABOUT THE AUTHOR

Jean Kinney Williams lives in Cincinnati with her husband Brian Williams and their four children. Her nonfiction books for children include *Matthew Henson: Polar Adventurer*, and a series of books about American religions, which included *The Amish, The Shakers, The Mormons, The Quakers* and *The Christian Scientists*. Ms. Williams is also the author of *Sandra Day O'Connor* in the Ferguson Career Biography series.

She enjoys spending time with her family and her goal is to write fiction for children and adults.